You Are There!

Ancient Greece 432 BC

Wendy Conklin, M.A.

Consultants

Timothy Rasinski, Ph.D.
Kent State University

Lori Oczkus, M.A.
Literacy Consultant

Publishing Credits

Rachelle Cracchiolo, M.S.Ed., *Publisher*
Conni Medina, M.A.Ed., *Managing Editor*
Dona Herweck Rice, *Series Developer*
Emily R. Smith, M.A.Ed., *Content Director*
Stephanie Bernard and Seth Rogers, *Editors*
Robin Erickson, *Multimedia Designer*

Image Credits: p.8 Antonios Karvelas/Dreamstime; pp.10, 18-19 North Wind Picture Archives; p.14 Sebastian423/Dreamstime.com; p.15 Werner Forman/Getty Images; p.20 World History Archive/Alamy; p.23 Alessandro0770/Dreamstime.com; pp.26–27 Darrell Gulin/Getty Images; All other images iStock and/or Shutterstock.

Library of Congress Cataloging-in-Publication Data

Name: Conklin, Wendy, author.
Title: You are there! : Ancient Greece 432 BC / Wendy Conklin, M.A.
Other titles: You are there, Ancient Greece 432 BC | Ancient Greece 432 BC
Description: Huntington Beach, CA : Teacher Created Materials, [2016] | Includes index. | Audience: Grades 4-6.
Identifiers: LCCN 2016012330 (print) | LCCN 2016012862 (ebook) | ISBN 9781493836000 (pbk.) | ISBN 9781480757042 (eBook)
Subjects: LCSH: Greece--History--To 146 B.C.--Juvenile literature. | Greece--Civilization--To 146 B.C.--Juvenile literature.
Classification: LCC DF77 .C6965 2016 (print) | LCC DF77 (ebook) | DDC 938/.02--dc23
LC record available at http://lccn.loc.gov/2016012330

Teacher Created Materials
5301 Oceanus Drive
Huntington Beach, CA 92649-1030
http://www.tcmpub.com

ISBN 978-1-4938-3600-0

Printed in Malaysia. THU001.8399

Table of Contents

Welcome to the Year 432 BC!

Sweet and spicy smells fill the air as I run down the stone path. The pavement is hard but smooth under my leather sandals. The vibrant sunlight makes the moist air heavy around me, and I start to sweat. I'm sprinting like our great Olympic athletes. Although I am not yet old enough to vote, one day I, Pericles, a son of Athens who is named for the great Greek statesman, will have my say in our Greek **democracy**. Until then, I want to learn and see all I can in trendsetting Greece.

Politics Is a Greek Thing

The Greek term for **city-state** is ***polis***. The modern-day word *politics* comes from *polis*.

Trendsetter for Democracy

You may have heard the term *city-state* before, but perhaps you don't know what it means. A city-state is formed when a city and nearby areas join together to form an independent state. This means they make their own laws and decisions, just as in a democracy. (As I said, Greece is a trendsetter!) This is the first time in history that any form of governing by the people has taken place. Athens and Sparta are the two most powerful city-states, but there are many other city-states, as well as colonies, established abroad.

Luckily for me, I live in the city-state of Athens. Citizens here have a right to stand up and voice opinions about the government. It doesn't matter if I grow up to become a farmer, an aristocrat, or a lowly laborer—all citizens' voices are equal. And we are wary of anyone who has too much power! We don't want a single person trying to sway others to his side because then he will have more **clout** than the rest of us. Recently, I witnessed leaders scratching the names of people with too much power on some ***ostraka***, old pieces of pottery. Anyone reaching 600 votes must leave Athens for 10 years.

Who Exactly Was a Citizen of Athens?

To be considered a citizen in Athens, a person had to be a male over 18 years of age and born in Athens. Earlier in the city-state's history, a person also had to own land to be a citizen.

At its core, *democracy* means that the people rule themselves. But in actuality, we elect people to rule for us. While this is a good way to govern overall, Athens does not have a perfect system. There are still injustices. For example, the rich Athenians have more advantages than the poor people do. Politicians do their best to sway the voters to their points of view, even if they are not right. If you are a woman, a slave, or from another city-state, you can't vote in Athens.

Sparta's democratic socicty, though, is not exactly like society in Athens. Instead, Spartans live under the rule of two kings, elders, judges, and an assembly of men. Free men elect the assembly. This group of men governs the city-state together.

Pericles, a Real Statesman

One of the greatest statesmen of Athens was Pericles, a leader for more than 30 years. Even though he was a nobleman, he wanted commoners (people not of noble birth) to have chances to hold office. Because of his leadership, male commoners were able to hold public office for the first time starting in 457 BC.

Only the Strong Live in Sparta

Spartans think that living a simple life is best. Above all things, they value courage, strength, and loyalty to their city-state. Spartans would rather die in battle than live after being defeated. Mothers even send their sons to battle saying, "Return with your shield or on it," which means either win or die trying.

If I lived in Sparta, I would have left my home at seven years old to train for the army—and it would have been the only job I ever knew. Spartan boys my age lie, steal, and cheat—but they'd better not get caught or they will be punished harshly! And they always have to be brave. As part of the training for the military, boys have to bathe in freezing rivers and walk barefoot for long distances in efforts to toughen them up.

The Woman's Place

For the most part, Greek women were supposed to stay out of the public eye. They could only go out to fetch water and tend to the family graves. But in Sparta, women could own property. They could also wear shorter skirts there, which allowed for freer movement.

Think Link

- Why was it better for women to live in Sparta than in other city-states?
- Why might Spartans have reasons to be proud?
- For what reasons would it be difficult to be a Spartan?

Spartan girls also have to be strong. When they grow up, they single-handedly run their homes. Their husbands live in the army barracks until they are 30, and sometimes the men are away at war. It is important to educate Spartan women because they make important decisions every day. Spartans treat their women well (which is quite uncommon in other city-states). So, if you are a girl, you might want to think about living in Sparta.

statue of a Spartan soldier

Greeks Are Good at War

It would make sense for the city-states to all get along. We live in the same region, we govern ourselves, and we have enough room to live comfortably. But, in truth, we are at war with one another almost constantly. And although the city-states fight one another regularly, the bigger threat to Greece in my day is actually Persia. The Persians want to extend their empire. They are richer, stronger, and more organized than my countrymen. We soon learn that there's nothing like being under threat to unite feuding city-states. We join together nobly in a few notable battles.

Here's Your Earth and Water

Some of the smaller city-states surrendered to the Persians. But when the Persians arrived in Sparta, they demanded the Spartans give them earth and water. This would serve as a sign of their submission to Persia. In response, the Spartans threw the men down a well. The Spartans made it clear that they would not submit to them.

ancient Olympic athletes

The First Marathon

The Persians set sail in 490 BC for Marathon, a town just north of Athens. The Athenian soldiers marched to meet them on the beach. My people were vastly outnumbered, but we won anyway. The defeated Persians ran toward Athens, which was unguarded. The Athenian soldiers were weighed down by armor and exhaustion. But they were able to march more than 40 kilometers (25 miles) back to Athens in only six hours. Then, my countrymen beat the Persians again! This was the very first **marathon**.

In another battle, a Greek traitor gave the Persians information about a secret route. The Persians traveled through the route and trapped some Spartans! Many brave Spartans died standing their ground. The Persians then turned to attack an Athenian fleet of ships. But my people defeated the Persians. After one last battle on land, we Greeks defeated the Persians for good!

Greek soldiers battling a Persian invasion

The Spartans Flex Their Muscles

Despite coming together, the Spartans wanted to make sure the Athenians didn't get too strong. Remember, city-states are always at war with one another. Before I was born, Sparta and its **allies** launched an attack on Athens. While Sparta had the stronger army, Athens had a strong wall to keep its enemies out. No matter how hard they tried, the Spartan army could not get through the wall.

Wars Lead to the Decline of Greece

The wars between the city-states, such as the Peloponnesian War, weakened Greece as a **civilization**. The wars helped other countries grow stronger, and eventually they became stronger than the city-states of Greece. Later, outsiders (such as Alexander the Great) attacked and dominated the Greeks.

Athens also had the benefit of its location. It is located near the shore. Athenians have an amazing fleet of warships called **triremes**. The boats can row right into the sides of enemy ships and split them in half! Having ships also allowed Athens to get supplies easily.

Everything seemed to be going in favor of my home city-state until our navy suffered a huge defeat to the Spartans. Then, the supplies stopped coming, so we had to open the gates to get food and water. That's when the Spartans took over Athens and won the war. We refer to this as the Peloponnesian War.

Pericles giving his famous Funeral Oration to the people of Athens

Oh, My Gods and Goddesses

Take my advice. You don't want the gods mad at you! While our gods help us at times, they can be selfish and fickle. They live lives of luxury on Mount Olympus, doing whatever they want to do. Yet, their actions directly affect our lives. When they are upset, we suffer the consequences. For example, Zeus throws lightning bolts that can kill people when he gets mad. We give offerings and make sacrifices to the gods to keep them happy. Many people keep **shrines** in their own homes where they make offerings and say prayers. Others do this at our temples. We not only want to keep the gods' anger in check, but we also need their help in everything, from making sure we have good harvests to guaranteeing that newborn children are healthy.

ruins of a temple

Do You Want to Be a Hero?

In Greek myths, a hero (or a demigod) is the child of a mortal and a god. Because of this, heroes have more empathy for humans than the gods do. They can also cross over into the heavenly world where the gods live. Some mythological heroes, such as Perseus and Theseus, spend their time killing dangerous beasts that threaten mortals.

Celebrations to Honor the Gods

The Greek year was filled with celebrations and holidays to honor the gods. They believed these festivals kept the gods happy and kept the people of Greece from feeling the gods' vengeance.

Getting to Know the Gods

You might be wondering, "Who are these mysterious gods living on Mount Olympus, drinking **nectar**, eating **ambrosia**, and ruling over the Greeks?" Many of the gods are related and have complicated relationships, to say the least. Zeus, the lord of the sky, is in charge of all the gods. Hera, his wife, is goddess of marriage and family, even though her own marriage and family are often in turmoil. Zeus has many children, but not all of them share the same mother. This is the cause of most of their problems!

Important Gods to Know

Original **Olympians**: These Olympians are the children of the Titans. Kronos is the ruler of the Titans and Rhea is his wife.	
Aphrodite	born fully grown when Kronos defeated his father; goddess of love and beauty
Demeter	daughter of Kronos and Rhea; goddess of the harvest
Hades*	son of Kronos and Rhea; god of the underworld
Hera	daughter of Kronos and Rhea; goddess of marriage and family
Hestia*	daughter of Kronos and Rhea; goddess of protecting the home; gave up her place on Mount Olympus to Dionysus
Poseidon	son of Kronos and Rhea; god of the sea
Zeus	youngest son of Kronos and Rhea; god of the sky; king of the gods

Second-generation Olympians: These Olympians are the children of the original Olympians.

Apollo	son of Zeus and the Titan Leto; god of the sun, light, music, and prophecy; twin brother of Artemis
Ares	son of Zeus and Hera; god of the violent aspects of war
Artemis	daughter of Zeus and the Titan Leto; goddess of the moon and the hunt; twin sister of Apollo
Athena	daughter of Zeus; goddess of wisdom, courage, inspiration, civilization, law and justice, strategic warfare, mathematics, strength, strategy, the arts, crafts, and skill
Dionysus	son of Zeus and a mortal woman named Semele; god of wine and the grape harvest
Hephaestus	son of Zeus and Hera; god of fire and metal working
Hermes	son of Zeus and the goddess Maia; god of travelers, merchants, and thieves; messenger of the gods
Persephone*	daughter of Zeus and Demeter; goddess of spring; queen of the underworld; tricked into becoming the wife of Hades

*Didn't live on Mount Olympus but still considered Olympians

Hermes

Games to Honor Zeus

Every year since 776 BC, we honor Zeus and other gods with a festival at Olympia. The top athletes from different city-states enter contests such as boxing matches and races. You can distinguish the trainers from the athletes by the long sticks the trainers carry to point out bad form or to give the athletes quick slaps for laziness. If you are a truly skilled athlete, you enter the pentathlon, which is composed of five events. At one point, all the runners put on armor weighing over 50 pounds and run four laps of the stadium. Many of them collapse before reaching the finish line. Of course, the biggest rivals are the Athenians and the Spartans. But all the city-states put aside their differences to compete.

No Women Allowed

Women were not allowed at the ancient Greek Olympics. In fact, the law stated that a married woman found in the crowd would be thrown off a cliff. But unmarried girls could attend the games. There were even races that honored Hera specifically for girls.

Olympia, site of the ancient Olympic Games

Let's make our way to the stadium in Olympia. It seats about 45,000 people, and there is not a bad view anywhere. We will sit on dirt seats, but the important members of Greek society make their way to the stone seats.

Look! The **pankration** is about to start. In this game, fighters can hit, kick, bite, and claw at each other's eyes. The last man alive wins the game. And you don't want to miss the exciting chariot races because there are some spectacular crashes to be seen!

Living the Greek Life

Life is probably very different where I live from where you do. Yet, much of what you have today is likely because of my people. Athenians of my day and long ago created **legacies** that will serve people for thousands of years.

Greek Thinkers

Some people in Athens are very wealthy, so they have time to sit and talk about ideas. On any given day, you can find Socrates, who was born around 470 BC, in the city square. He constantly poses questions about virtue and religion. Government officials don't like him much, though. This is probably because he has a huge following. And he doesn't always agree with the government's forms of justice. But Socrates isn't the only great thinker.

Other Greek Notables

Aristarchus was the first person to claim that Earth rotates and revolves around the sun. He also tried to measure the distance between the sun, moon, and Earth. Another Greek, Euclid, was the first person to state that the shortest distance between two places is a straight line.

Euclid

Thanks to Pythagoras, who was born around 570 BC, I know how to find the measurement of the third side of a right triangle. Other civilizations used the ideas of the **Pythagorean theorem** ($a^2 + b^2 = c^2$). But Pythagoras was the first to prove that it works.

Hippocrates was born in 460 BC. He recognized the symptoms of epilepsy and pneumonia. When we wondered how to be healthier, he was the one who said we needed to eat right, exercise, sleep, and stay clean.

Socrates

Socrates and Plato Make a Mark

Socrates was arrested in 399 BC and was sentenced to death for treason and **corrupting** young people. His most famous student was Plato, who founded the first university-type school in Athens. The scientist and philosopher, Aristotle, was a student at this school as well.

Plato

Amazing Art and Architecture

Take a look around Greece! You will see many carved statues and gleaming white temples. Believe it or not, the government hires and pays artists to create beautiful works like these. During our visit to Olympia, you probably saw the Colossal Zeus statue. You might have noticed that the statue barely fits inside the temple built for it!

Many Greeks enjoy going to our amazing theater at Epidaurus to see **comedies** and **tragedies** performed. With 13,000 seats, I can always find a good spot. Even if I sit in the farthest seat away from the stage, I can still hear the actors tear a piece of paper. The **acoustics** are that amazing! Being an actor can be dangerous, though. If we don't like the play, we throw fruit and stones at the actors.

You can't help but notice the temples around Athens, the Parthenon in particular. These temples are basic rectangles, but our architects figured out how to design columns that can hold up the weight of the stone roofs. These columns are incredible! First, our architects designed thick **Doric columns**. Then, **Ionic columns** became the fad, and then fancy **Corinthian columns** showed up. Other civilizations will definitely want to copy these!

Wonder of the Ancient World

The Colossal Zeus statue in Olympia was completed in 430 BC by the famous Athenian sculptor Phidias. But in AD 391, a Christian emperor closed the temples and banned the Olympic Games. The statue was moved to Constantinople, only to have it be destroyed by fire a few years later.

A Dinner Invitation

The temples are a far cry from our simple homes built of mud bricks. My house has a courtyard in the middle (as most houses do), with rooms that surround it. Greek homes made out of mud may not be pretty, but they are practical—keeping us cool in summer and warm in winter.

I'm fortunate, though; my father has the very respected job of farming (instead of working in a lowly factory in Athens). He, along with our slaves, works the land to raise wheat and **barley**. Come over tonight and have dinner with my family. We will enjoy the usual meal—wine, figs, olives, grapes, and bread baked with wheat from our own fields. My father is making a sacrifice of a goat to the gods, so we will also get to enjoy what's left over.

Be sure to wear your best **tunic** tonight. I'll definitely be wearing my new wool tunic. My best dog will meet you at the door, where you can take your sandals off. You won't need them because we all go barefoot in the house. Our house slave will take care of you, and if the need arises, we do have a flushing toilet—thank goodness for technology! The **aqueducts** bring the clean water into the city, and clay pipes pump it right into our home.

Slaves, All Too Common

Most Greeks owned slaves during ancient times. Many slaves were captured as prisoners of war, and others were kidnapped from conquered places. If families were deep in debt, they sometimes sold members of their families into slavery to pay off the debts. Families that couldn't take care of babies sometimes left them outside, where they were found by slave owners and raised as slaves.

figs and barley

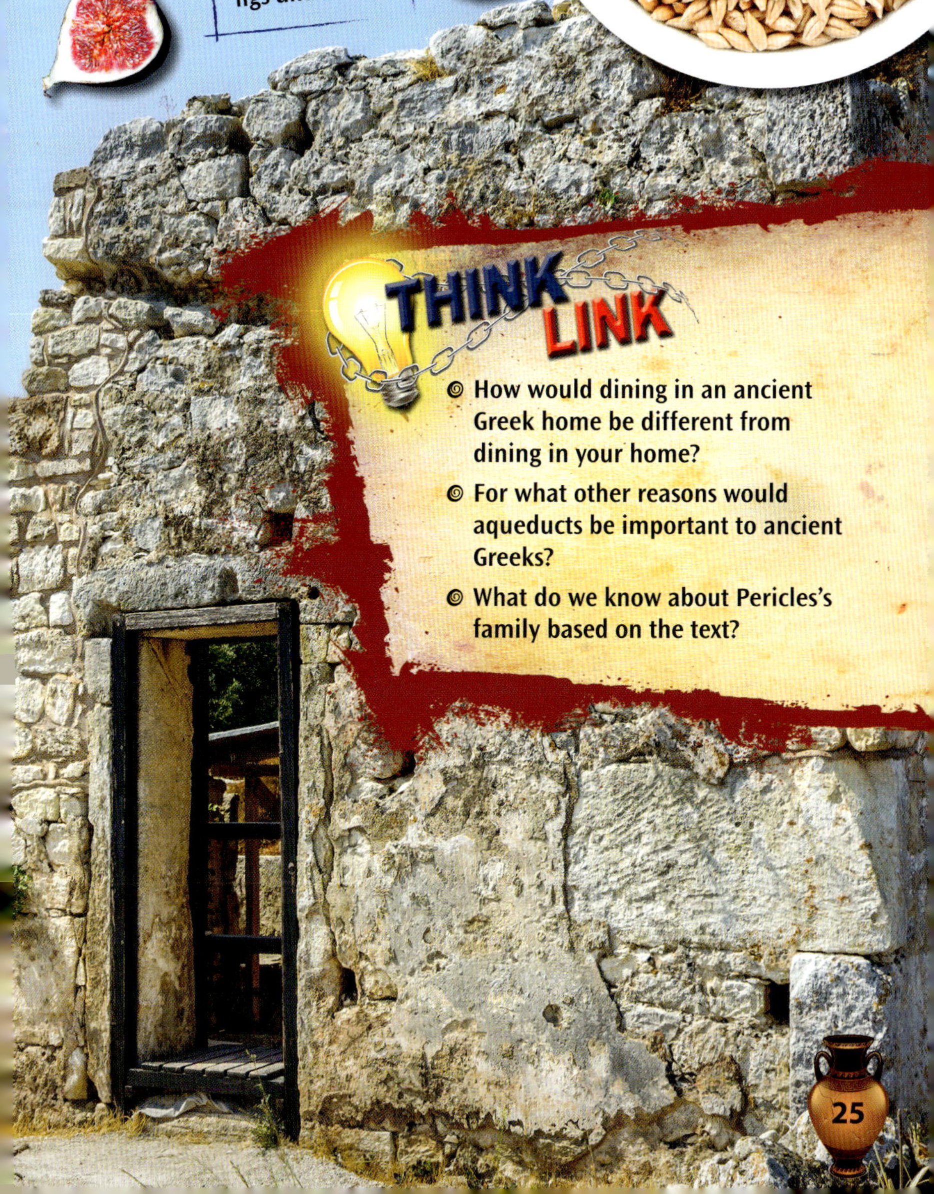

THINK LINK

- How would dining in an ancient Greek home be different from dining in your home?
- For what other reasons would aqueducts be important to ancient Greeks?
- What do we know about Pericles's family based on the text?

It's All Greek to Me

Friend, I'm glad you stopped by and inquired about my homeland. As you can see, we Greeks are quite advanced in many areas, including the way we govern, our religious beliefs, our technology, and our thirst for knowledge.

The Greek Alphabet

The Greeks were not the first to use an alphabet—that was the Phoenicians—but they were the first to assign vowel sounds to letters. Many words today are influenced by these old Greek symbols.

Before you go, here are a few final pieces of advice. First, don't anger the gods unless you are prepared to absorb their vengeance. Countless stories tell how most mortals don't survive the gods' fury. Second, look for examples of where our government has influenced others. I guarantee that some form of our democracy will last through the ages. Third, when you are in school learning how to question and think, be grateful. Amazing Greeks, such as Socrates, created ways of thinking and questioning that will be used for a long time. Finally, appreciate the art that is around you. Artisans spend so much of their time creating amazing columns, buildings, sculptures, and everyday vases. Someone influenced these artists—and it was probably the Greeks!

The First Real Readers

Greek society was the first in which a large amount of the population could read. In spite of the influence of books and the many great Greek philosophers, most Greeks did not enjoy learning from books. Some Greeks encouraged people to be attentive to what was happening around them rather than what could be read in books.

Glossary

acoustics—the qualities in an area that help people hear sounds clearly

allies—groups that fight together during battles or a war

ambrosia—food of the gods

aqueducts—pipes used to carry water to the cities of ancient Greece

barley—grain used for food

city-state—an independent state formed when cities and nearby areas join together

civilization—a well-organized and clearly developed society

clout—power or influence

comedies—plays with funny themes that usually end happily

Corinthian columns—an ornate column that looks similar to leaves and flowers

corrupting—causing someone to become dishonest

democracy—a system of government in which the people choose leaders

Doric columns—a thick, heavy, plain column used on Greek buildings

Ionic columns—a column with scroll-shaped ornaments at the top

legacies—things passed down from ancestors

marathon—a race that is based on the long march made by the Athenians in ancient Greece

nectar—sweet syrup produced from flowers; drink of the gods

Olympians—gods who lived on Mount Olympus

ostraka (OS-truh-kuh)—pottery shards used by the assembly to ostracize members of the government that have too much power

pankration (pahn-CRAY-shun)—a sport that was a combination of boxing and wrestling

polis (POH-luhs)—the Greek word for city used to describe city-states

Pythagorean theorem—the square of the longest side of a right triangle is equal to the sum of the squares of the lengths of the other two sides

shrines—a place where people go to worship

tragedies—plays about conflicts that end sadly

triremes (TRY-reems)—Greek warships rowed by three banks of oarsmen

tunic—a gown-like garment that drapes over and is tied with a belt

Index

Check It Out!

Books

Clare, John D. 2005. *Ancient Greece: Historic Civilizations*. Gareth Stevens Publishing.

D'Aulaire, Edgar, and Ingri D'Aulaire. 1992. *D'Aulaires' Book of Greek Myths*. Delacorte Press.

Macdonald, Fiona. 2007. *You Wouldn't Want to Be a Slave in Ancient Greece!* Franklin Watts.

Pearson, Anne. 2000. *Eyewitness: Ancient Greece*. DK Publishing.

Riordan, Rick. 2006. *Percy Jackson and the Olympians: The Lightning Thief*. Disney Hyperion Books.

Videos

Kultur Video. *Ancient Greece: A Journey Back in Time (Lost Treasures of the Ancient World)*. Cromwell Productions.

Websites

A&E Television Network. *Ancient Greece*. http://www.history.com

University Press. *Ancient Greece*. http://www.ancientgreece.com

Try It!

Imagine waking up to find that you are suddenly living in ancient Greece! The only way for you to explain what happened to everyone back home is through a letter or visual presentation. You just have to hope it survives the thousands of years until present day. What will you tell your friends and family? Decide on the best way to share all the important details of your plan:

- What are some of the things you see? Include any famous landmarks.
- Where exactly in ancient Greece are you? What is it like there?
- Have you seen any famous people from the time period? Who? What happened?
- What is your role in society? Are you a soldier? A scholar?

About the Author

Wendy Conklin has been an educator for nearly 25 years, much of them as a prolific author and speaker. She has lived in Jerusalem, Chicago, and St. Louis, and currently lives in Round Rock, Texas, where she and her husband are raising two teenage girls and two middle-age dogs.